The Genius Of THE ANCIENT GREEKS

INNOVATIONS FROM PAST CIVILIZATIONS

IZZI HOWELL

CRABTREE
PUBLISHING COMPANY
WWW.CRABTREEBOOKS.COM

CRABTREE
PUBLISHING COMPANY
WWW.CRABTREEBOOKS.COM

Published in Canada
Crabtree Publishing
616 Welland Avenue
St. Catharines, ON
L2M 5V6

Published in the United States
Crabtree Publishing
PMB 59051
350 Fifth Ave, 59th Floor
New York, NY 10118

Published in 2020 by Crabtree Publishing Company

First published in Great Britain in 2019 by The Watts Publishing Group
Copyright © The Watts Publishing Group 2019

Author: Izzi Howell

Editorial director: Kathy Middleton

Editors: Izzi Howell, Petrice Custance

Proofreader: Melissa Boyce

Series Designer: Rocket Design (East Anglia) Ltd

Designer: Clare Nicholas

Prepress technician: Tammy McGarr

Print coordinator: Katherine Berti

Consultant: Philip Parker

Printed in the U.S.A./072019/CG20190501

Photo credits:
Alamy: North Wind Picture Archives 7b, De Luan 11t, Granger Historical Picture Archive 11b, Universal Images Group North America LLC 15, Heritage Image Partnership Ltd 19b, Greek photonews 23b; Getty: Richmatts cover and 17b, argalis 8, dimitris_k 10 and 30, ilbusca 17t, ZU_09 19t, VCG Wilson/Corbis 20b, Encyclopaedia Britannica/UIG 23t, imagestock 25t; Metropolitan Museum: The Bothmer Purchase Fund, 1978 5t, Fletcher Fund, 1938 13t, Fletcher Fund, 1931 3t and 20t, Rogers Fund, 1911 21, Rogers Fund, 1913 27t, Rogers Fund, 1916 29t; Shutterstock: Samot 5b, vivooo 6, Josep Curto 7t, Kamira 9t, Peter Hermes Furian 9b, Patalakha Sergii 12, Panos Karas 13b, Vdant85 14t, Marius G 14b, RossHelen 16, baldovina 18, EDUARDO AUSTREGESILO 22, Lefteris Papaulakis 3b , 24 and 27b, brulove 25bl, ulrich22 25bc, Kovaleva_Ka 25br, Alfio Ferlito 26, Aerial-motion 28, ANCH 29b and 31.

All design elements from Shutterstock.

Every attempt has been made to clear copyright. Should there be any inadvertent omission please apply to the publisher for rectification.

The website addresses (URLs) included in this book were valid at the time of going to press. However, it is possible that contents or addresses may have changed since the publication of this book. No responsibility for any such changes can be accepted by either the author or the Publisher.

Library and Archives Canada Cataloguing in Publication

Title: The genius of the ancient Greeks / Izzi Howell.
Names: Howell, Izzi, author.
Series: Genius of the ancients.
Description: Series statement: The genius of the ancients | Includes index.
Identifiers: Canadiana (print) 2019010824X | Canadiana (ebook) 20190108274 | ISBN 9780778765721 (hardcover) | ISBN 9780778765929 (softcover) | ISBN 9781427123893 (HTML)
Subjects: LCSH: Greece—Civilization—To 146 B.C.—Juvenile literature. | LCSH: Technological innovations—Greece—History—To 1500—Juvenile literature. | LCSH: Greece—Civilization—Juvenile literature. | LCSH: Greece—Antiquities—Juvenile literature. | LCSH: Technological innovations— Greece—Juvenile literature.
Classification: LCC DF77 .H69 2019 | DDC j938—dc23

Library of Congress Cataloging-in-Publication Data

Names: Howell, Izzi, author.
Title: The genius of the ancient Greeks / Izzi Howell.
Description: New York, New York : Crabtree Publishing Company, 2020. Series: The genius of the ancients | Audience: Ages 9-12. | Audience: Grades: 4-6. | Includes index. |
Identifiers: LCCN 2019014235 (print) | LCCN 2019018673 (ebook) | ISBN 9781427123893 (Electronic) | ISBN 9780778765721 (hardcover) | ISBN 9780778765929 (pbk.)
Subjects: LCSH: Greece--Civilization--Juvenile literature. | Greece--Antiquities--Juvenile literature. | Technological innovations--Greece--Juvenile literature.
Classification: LCC DF77 (ebook) | LCC DF77 .H69 2020 (print) | DDC 938--dc23
LC record available at https://lccn.loc.gov/2019014235

CONTENTS

THE ANCIENT GREEKS

Who?

The first great Greek civilizations were the Minoans, who lived on the island of Crete from 3000 to 1450 B.C.E., and the Mycenaeans, who lived on mainland Greece from 1650 to 1100 B.C.E. After the Mycenaeans, Greece entered a 300-year period known as the Dark Ages. No one is sure why, but the Greeks of the Dark Ages stopped writing, creating detailed artworks, and building large settlements.

Bulls were very important in Minoan **culture**. This stone carving was found in a palace in Knossos, Crete.

Around 800 B.C.E., small villages began to grow into cities. Each city became a separate city-state, controlled by its own ruler. This is partly because Greece's geography of islands and mountains physically separated different areas, so they developed independently. During this time, known as the Archaic period, a more advanced civilization started to return to Greece.

This map shows some of the important places and city-states in ancient Greece. There were over 1,000 city-states across the Greek world.

MACEDONIA

Mount Olympus △

Troy

AEGEAN SEA

Delphi

ATTICA

Thebes
Salamis
Corinth
Olympia
Mycenae
Argos
Cape Sounion

Athens

Ephesus

Miletus

Delos

Pylos
Sparta

IONIAN SEA

Knossos

CRETE

MEDITERRANEAN SEA

The height of the ancient Greek civilization was the Classical period, from 508 to 323 B.C.E. This was a time of **innovations**, scientific discoveries, new ideas about **philosophy** and theater, and the beginnings of **democracy**. During the Hellenistic period, 323 to 30 B.C.E., the ancient Greeks controlled a huge territory across the Mediterranean and the Middle East.

This jar was given as a prize during the **Panathenaic Games**, in which different city-states competed against each other (see pages 28–29).

What happened?

Beginning around 146 B.C.E., the Romans and other groups started to take control of Greece and Greek territories. The civilizations that took over the Greek world were highly influenced by many aspects of Greek culture, including science and literature. The **legacy** of ancient Greece can be seen today around the world, in modern politics, **architecture**, and language.

The remains of this temple can be seen in Delphi, Greece. There are ruins of many ancient Greek buildings across Europe and the Middle East.

CITY-STATES

Ancient Greece was not one country politically. It was divided into small **city-states**, such as Athens, Sparta, and Corinth. Although people across Greece spoke the same language and followed the same religion, people considered themselves Athenians or Spartans, rather than Greeks.

GENIUS
★ ORGANIZED COMMUNITIES ★

Local identities

Many different social groups lived in each city-state, including citizens, or people born in the city-state, non-citizens, and enslaved people. All social groups shared a common city-state identity. Citizens, especially male citizens, enjoyed the most freedom and often gathered in special meeting places, such as the **agora**.

The agora in Athens sat at the foot of the **Acropolis**. The remains of the agora are open to visitors today.

Different rulers

City-states were ruled in different ways, such as **monarchies** or **oligarchies**. Eventually, one city-state developed a style of ruling that worked particularly well. In 508 B.C.E., the city-state of Athens became a democracy. Men who were born in Athens and who were over 20 years old could vote and make decisions on how the city-state was run.

At war

City-states fought each other to show power and to gain new territory. The most famous war between city-states was the Peloponnesian War between Athens and Sparta, from 431 to 404 B.C.E. Almost every Greek city-state joined in the war, which was finally won by Sparta. City-states also worked together to fight a common enemy. From 492 to 449 B.C.E., several city-states fought in a war against the **Persian Empire**.

City-states, including Athens, Corinth, and Megara, came together to fight against the Persian Empire, which was trying to conquer Greek territory. Greece won the war.

THE GREEK WORLD

Sometime between 900 and 800 B.C.E., ancient Greek city-states began to set up new **colonies** outside Greece. They chose areas with **fertile** land for farming and access to various **natural resources**.

GENIUS ★ NEW TERRITORY ★

Exchanging ideas

City-states set up colonies around the Mediterranean Sea and across Europe, in areas known today as Italy, France, Spain, and North Africa. Settlers spread ancient Greek culture and **customs** to these new territories. They also learned from and were influenced by the people living in these areas.

Greek settlers introduced typical Greek structures to their colonies, such as this theater in Syracuse, Italy.

TEST of TIME

Many modern cities started out as new settlements in Greek colonies. For example, settlers from the Greek island of Rhodes established the port of Neapolis in Italy, which is now the city of Naples. The colony of Massilia, begun by settlers from a Greek city-state in Turkey, is now the French city of Marseille.

Alexander's empire

Alexander the Great was the king of the city-state of Macedonia. In 334 B.C.E., he began conquering huge areas of territory across Egypt, Syria, Iraq, Turkey, and India. Eventually, he controlled an empire of over 2 million square miles (5.2 million square km).

This marble head of Alexander the Great was once attached to the body of a full statue.

WOW!

Alexander the Great never lost a single battle!

A new age

Alexander the Great's giant empire marked the beginning of the age of Hellenistic Greece. The ancient Greek language and customs spread across the Mediterranean and Middle East, and mixed with the culture of newly conquered areas. For example, in Egypt, the new Greek rulers called themselves **pharaohs** to please the Egyptian people.

This map shows Alexander's empire at its greatest size in 323 B.C.E.

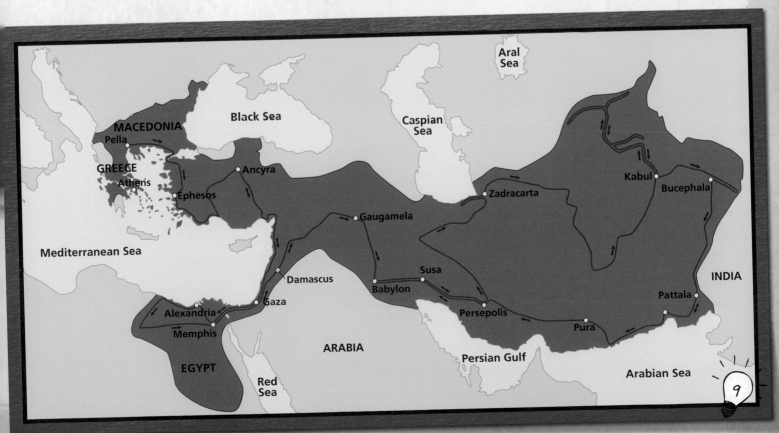

DEMOCRACY

Beginning in 508 B.C.E., the city-state of Athens developed a new form of government. It was called democracy, which comes from a Greek word meaning rule by the people. Today, many governments around the world are democracies.

GENIUS ★ PEOPLE POWER

Male voters

Even though democracy meant rule by the people, only male citizens of Athens could vote. Women, enslaved people, or people from other city-states were not allowed to take part. Male voters could attend meetings almost weekly to choose new leaders and decide how to punish crimes or whether to go to war. They voted with a show of hands, and the majority won the vote. This is unlike modern democracy, in which people elect representatives to make decisions on their behalf.

Meetings took place on the Pnyx, a hill in Athens. Voters would sit on this hill and listen to speakers.

Keeping things fair

A council of 500 men, known as the Boule, was in charge of running the city-state. Members of the Boule were chosen **randomly** by drawing numbers. They were only allowed to serve for one year, and never more than twice in their lifetime. This was considered the fairest way to have an even selection of men from across the city-state. Holding elections would have given well-known or wealthy men an advantage.

The members of the Boule attended meetings almost every day.

(((BRAIN WAVE)))

Voters could vote to banish dangerous leaders who were too ambitious or power-hungry. To do this, men carved the name of the politician on a shard of pottery called an ostrakon. If enough people voted, the leader could be sent away from the city for 10 years. *Ostrakon* is the root of the modern word ostracize, which means to exclude.

WARFARE

GENIUS ★ ORGANIZED SOLDIERS

Organization was an important factor in the success of Greek armies. Soldiers were well trained and knew how to work and move together on the battlefield.

Hoplites

The ancient Greek army was mainly made up of foot soldiers called hoplites. They fought in organized groups called phalanxes. In a phalanx, hoplites stood in close rows with their round shields locked together for protection. The first rows held their spears horizontally to stop the enemy from getting close. When the phalanx marched together, it was very hard for the enemy to break through.

The word phalanx is still used today to describe a group of people standing or moving closely together.

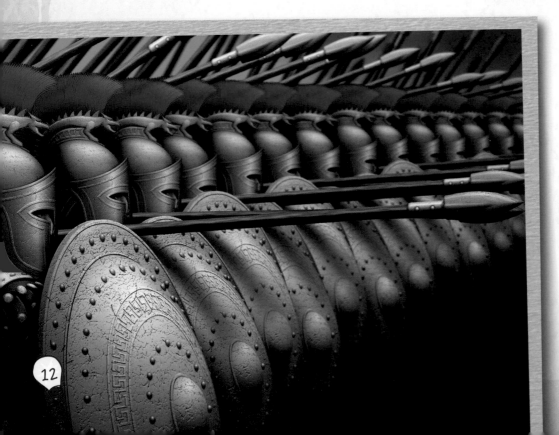

Hoplites in a phalanx **formation.** Each hoplite provided his own equipment, which included a shield, a spear, a metal helmet, and armor.

Training soldiers

The city-state of Sparta was famous for its military training. Boys left their families and trained as soldiers from the age of seven. During training, soldiers weren't given enough food to eat or warm clothes to wear, as it was believed that this made them strong. The training seemed to work, as Spartan soldiers were famous for their fierce fighting spirit.

Ancient Greek soldiers fought with metal-tipped spears. They used a short sword for close-up fighting.

Spotting weaknesses

Alexander the Great was well known for his excellent battle tactics. He identified his enemies' weaknesses and organized his troops to attack them where they were vulnerable. This helped him to beat armies that were much larger than his own.

This modern statue of Alexander the Great riding his horse Bucephalus stands in the city of Thessaloniki, Greece. Soldiers on horseback became an important part of ancient Greek armies.

(((BRAIN WAVE)))

One of Alexander's best **tactical** victories was at the Battle of Gaugamela in 331 B.C.E. Alexander beat the Persian king Darius III, even though Darius had a larger army and chose the fighting ground to his advantage. Alexander won by drawing the sides of the enemy's army into battle so that the middle, where Darius was, was left exposed. In the end, the Persian army retreated.

13

SHIPS

The ancient Greeks used ships for trade and transport. They were also important weapons, used to defend Greek territory against invasion.

GENIUS ★ SMASHING SHIPS

Smooth sailing

Ships were an obvious choice to transport cargo between Greece's many islands and territory outside the mainland. Sailing was often easier than traveling across land, as much of Greece is rocky and mountainous. Ships used for trading were powered by sails.

Trading ships sailed close to shore so as not to get lost.

(((BRAIN WAVE)))

At Corinth, there is a narrow land bridge that links the north and south parts of Greece. Ships had to sail all the way around the south of Greece to get from one side to the other, which took a long time. To solve this problem, the ancient Greeks built the Diolkos, a stone track over the narrow piece of land. The ships' cargo, and even the ships themselves, could be pulled across the track to the other side. Today, there is a canal for ships.

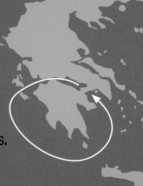

Rowing into battle

Ancient Greek warships were called triremes. They were very lightweight, with three rows of oars on each side. The oars overlapped at different levels so as not to waste space. In battle, sailors rowed the triremes at superfast speeds, and could easily move the ship in the direction they wanted to travel.

The overlapping oars of a trireme were below deck, which kept the top deck clear for fighting. After an enemy ship was rammed, sailors often jumped onto the trireme to continue the battle.

Crash!

The ancient Greeks didn't have effective weapons that could be used to attack other ships from a distance. Instead, they rowed their trireme right up to an enemy ship and crashed into it with the bronze tip of the boat, which acted as a ram. This made a hole in the enemy ship, breaking it apart or sinking it.

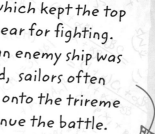

15

ARCHITECTURE

Ancient Greek architecture was simple yet sophisticated. Architects followed sets of rules when designing buildings, which meant that many buildings were built in a similar style.

GENIUS ★ ORDERED DESIGN

Shape and material

Nearly all Greek buildings were rectangular, with columns inside to support the roof. The first buildings were made of wood. Later, marble and limestone were used for many grand public buildings. Both of these stones are easily found across Greece.

TEST OF TIME

Ancient Greek architecture has inspired many architects throughout history, from Roman times up until the present day. You can see Greek-inspired buildings in most modern cities.

At the remains of the Temple of Olympian Zeus in Athens, the beams that supported the roof can still be seen at the top of the columns.

Different styles

Balance, order, and symmetry were very important to Greek architects. They developed three different styles of architecture, called Doric, Ionic, and Corinthian. Most ancient Greek buildings were built in one of these three styles. For this reason, many buildings look alike.

The differences between Doric, Ionic, and Corinthian buildings are most obvious in the style of their columns.

Ionic

scrolled top

24 sides

plain top

20 sides

finely decorated top with leaves and scrolls

Corinthian

24 sides

large base

Doric

no base

small base

Seen from afar

Grand ancient Greek buildings, such as temples, were designed to be admired from far away. Architects learned tricks to make these large buildings look more visually appealing from a distance. They made columns slightly thicker at the bottom and positioned them to lean slightly inward. The corner columns were also made slightly larger. When seen from far away, this creates an **optical illusion** that every line of the building is perfectly straight.

The Parthenon temple was built on the Acropolis in the center of Athens, so that it could be seen from across the city.

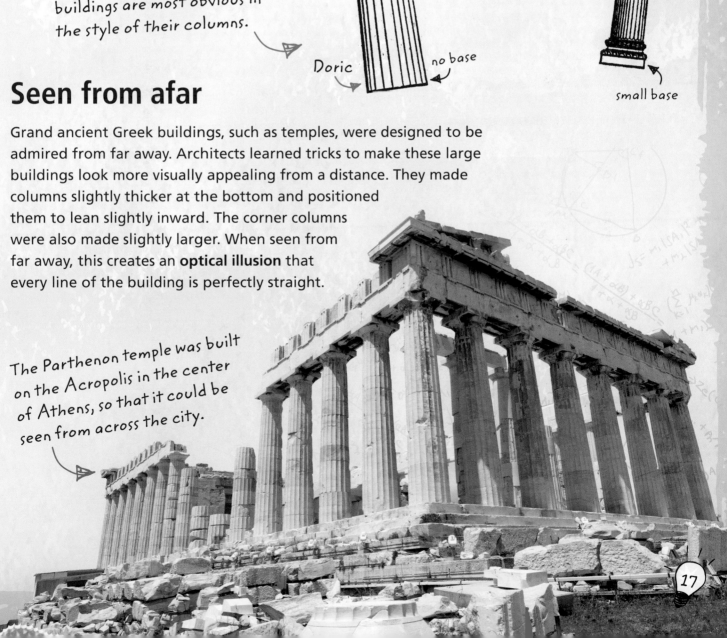

17

WRITING

The legacy of ancient Greek writing lives on today through its alphabet. Written records of Greek ideas about science, mathematics, and philosophy have influenced many great thinkers.

GENIUS ★ RECORD-KEEPING

A new alphabet

The ancient Greek alphabet developed around 800 B.C.E. It was based on the **Phoenician** alphabet, but the Greeks added new letters for vowels. This allowed them to write words that more closely represented the sounds of spoken words. The Greek alphabet was passed on to other groups, including the Romans, and is still used in Greece today.

There are many examples of ancient Greek text carved into stone, such as this law code engraved on a public building in Gortyn, Crete. Every other line of the text is written backwards, which was a common style of public writing.

TEST OF TIME

Today, Greek letters are used as symbols in math and science. The symbol for the Greek letter *pi* (π) is used to represent the number 3.14. This number is the result of dividing a circle's circumference, or distance around, by its diameter, or distance across.

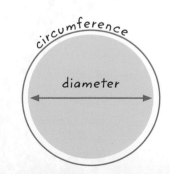

circumference

diameter

Types of text

Many Greek texts survive to this day, including accounts of historical events and exploration, and books about philosophy, science, medicine, **astronomy**, and math. We can also read ancient Greek epic stories, such as The Iliad and The Odyssey. These stories tell the tale of the **Trojan War** and the journey home of the hero Odysseus. They are fictional, but may have been partly based on real events.

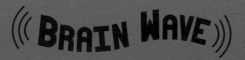

(((BRAIN WAVE)))

Before the Greek Classical period, most accounts of history were a mixture of fact and fiction, combining elements from **myths** and real events. Greek historians, such as Herodotus, took a new approach and started to record events as accurately as possible. This inspired later historians to do the same.

In *The Odyssey*, Odysseus has to escape from a cyclops, or a mythical one-eyed giant.

The Alexandria library

One of the largest libraries in the ancient world was located in the city of Alexandria, in Greek-controlled Egypt. The library contained Greek books and foreign texts, so visitors had access to many new ideas all in one place. Later, the library burned down and the texts were lost forever. It is only because translations of these texts had been made into other languages that we know about them today.

This drawing from the 1800s suggests what it would have been like inside the Library of Alexandria. Visitors are reading from the library's collection of **papyrus** scrolls.

ART

From the beginning of ancient Greek civilization, the human body was the inspiration for their art. They developed different ways to represent the body in art, which can be seen in the pottery and sculptures that survive today.

Different bodies

The ancient Greeks wanted the human body to look as lifelike as possible in their art. They showed people doing a range of activities and in many different poses. The human body was often shown naked, as the Greeks believed this showed the model as a hero.

This vase is painted with images of women weaving. Historians look at art to learn about everyday life and activities in ancient Greece.

Painting pottery

The ancient Greeks used plain pottery pots to store and transport liquids, such as wine or oil. They also produced elaborately painted pottery as pieces of art. Ancient Greek pottery was usually painted in just a few different colors. This made the designs stand out. Painters used delicate, precise lines to show the details. They often added patterns for decoration.

This Minoan pot is decorated with a detailed painting of an octopus.

Skilled sculptors

Highly skilled ancient Greek sculptors used tiny chisels to carve delicate details that brought their sculptures to life. Every detail in the human body was recreated in stone.

This ancient Greek sculpture is full of details, from the creases in the skin on the hands to the folds of the clothing.

WOW!

Ancient Greek sculptures were originally painted in bright colors! They look plain today because the paint has worn away over time.

TEST of TIME

During the **European Renaissance**, artists such as Michelangelo were inspired by ancient Greek art. They captured the details of the human body, and made their artworks full of movement.

ASTRONOMY

Many ancient civilizations, such as the Egyptians and Babylonians, used the movements of the Sun and the planets to keep track of time. However, the ancient Greeks wanted to take it a step further and understand what they saw in the stars and why.

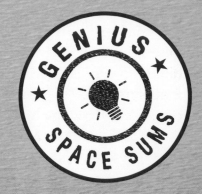

GENIUS ★ SPACE SUMS

During lunar **eclipses**, ancient Greek astronomers saw the circular shadow of Earth projected on to the Moon, which confirmed their theory of a round Earth.

Observation and explanation

The ancient Greeks began by closely observing the sky and coming up with theories that explained what they saw. For example, based on their observation that ships disappear as they move toward the horizon, they correctly figured out that Earth was round, and not flat as some believed. They also noticed that stars appear to move higher in the sky as you move toward the south, which suggests that Earth is curved.

Geometry

Astronomers used geometry, or the math of shapes, to work out the **dimensions** of Earth. The astronomer Eratosthenes calculated Earth's circumference by measuring the angle of the Sun in the sky in two different Egyptian cities. The Sun was directly above one city at noon, but not quite as high in another at the same time. He then measured the distance between the two cities and used these figures to work out the circumference. He was not exactly correct, but very close!

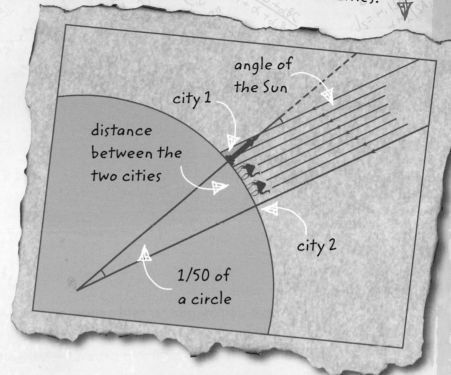

Eratosthenes worked out that the circumference of Earth was about 50 times the distance between the two cities.

angle of the Sun

city 1

distance between the two cities

city 2

1/50 of a circle

New instruments

Ancient Greek astronomers developed new tools to help them with their research. The astrolabe was an instrument that measured the angles of objects in space in **relation** to each other, which helped astronomers understand their movements. The Antikythera mechanism was a clockwork machine made of bronze. It contained moving dials and gears that calculated the positions of the stars and the Sun and predicted eclipses.

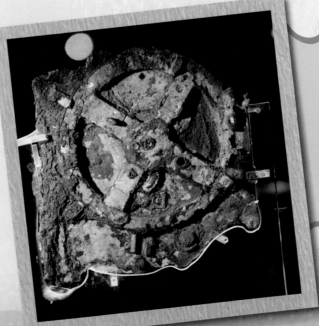

The remains of the Antikythera mechanism were found in a shipwreck off the coast of the Greek island Antikythera in 1901.

WOW!

The Antikythera mechanism is sometimes called the world's first computer!

MEDICINE

Ancient Greek doctors used ideas taken from philosophy, such as looking for **logical** answers, to try to better understand the human body. Their ideas influenced medicine for thousands of years afterward, and still do today.

GENIUS ★ **RATIONAL REMEDIES** ★

Natural causes and cures

The early ancient Greeks believed that diseases were caused by bad luck and could be cured by praying or pleasing the gods. This changed when ancient Greek doctors began trying to understand how the human body works in order to find logical causes and cures for diseases.

Early ancient Greeks prayed to Asclepius, the god of medicine, to cure their diseases. His stick and snake are used as a symbol to represent medicine today.

WOW!

Ancient Greek doctors were some of the first to observe and try to treat conditions such as diabetes and intestinal worms!

In balance

The ancient Greek doctor Hippocrates put forward the theory that the human body contained four substances—blood, phlegm, yellow bile, and black bile. He suggested that too much or too little of one substance caused illness. To cure illnesses, doctors tried to balance the substances— for example, by bleeding a patient they believed had too much blood. Although this theory was not correct, it was an important early example of doctors trying to logically understand and treat disease.

Ancient Greek doctors examined patients and observed their symptoms to try to understand what was wrong.

To cure patients with too much phlegm, doctors gave them barley soup, vinegar, and honey.

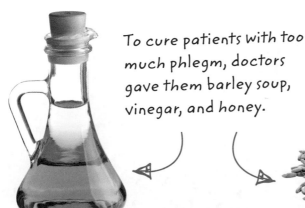

TEST of TIME

Modern doctors have to promise to keep patients' medical history a secret and to try their best to help them. This is known as the Hippocratic Oath and dates back to Hippocrates's ideas about how doctors should behave.

THEATER

Ancient Greek plays were held in front of very large audiences. Special techniques were developed to help everyone follow what was happening onstage.

GENIUS
★ AUDIENCE ACOUSTICS ★

Shape and space

Greek theaters were built in a semicircular shape with **tiered** seating, so that everyone could see what was happening onstage. Actors performed on a raised stage in the center. In front of this stage was a flat area where members of the chorus performed. The chorus sang and danced, commenting on the events of the play.

The limestone seats at Epidaurus help block background noise, such as talking in the audience.

(((BRAIN WAVE)))

The theater at Epidaurus has excellent **acoustics**, which help the audience hear the actors clearly. The steps of limestone seats help the sound of the actors' voices travel throughout the theater. Historians aren't sure if this design was accidental or done on purpose. However, it worked so well that the Greeks copied it in other theaters.

Comedies and tragedies

Greek plays were often comedies or tragedies. Comedies were funny and rude, with silly jokes and stereotypical characters. Tragedies were sad stories, which often presented a moral lesson about what is right or wrong. Playwrights wrote new plays for drama festivals, the very best of which were given prizes.

This pottery figure dating from ancient Greece represents a stereotypical old woman character from a Greek comedy. This type of character appeared in many Greek comedies.

WOW!

A wooden crane was sometimes used onstage to allow actors playing gods to fly through the air.

Masks

Greek actors often wore masks with exaggerated facial expressions. This helped faraway audience members to see how the characters were feeling. It also meant that actors could quickly and easily change roles without confusing the audience.

This is a stone model of a typical Greek mask. No original Greek masks survive today, as they were made from painted fabric that has **decomposed**. However, we know what the masks look like from models made in other materials.

SPORTS

GENIUS ★ CITY-STATE COMPETITION ★

There were at least four sports festivals in ancient Greece, the most famous of which were the Olympic Games at Olympia. The first Olympic Games were held in 776 B.C.E. as part of a religious festival. Over time, they became more political, as city-states sent representatives to compete away from the battlefield.

Calling a truce

One month before the Olympic Games, messengers traveled across the Greek world, spreading news of the upcoming games. Any wars or disputes between city-states were put on hold. The **truce** meant that athletes from different city-states could safely travel to and from Olympia, without fear of attack.

Events

The first Olympic Games lasted for just one day, with running races as the only events. Later, more events were added and the Olympic Games were extended to last five days. These events included **chariot** and horse racing, wrestling, boxing, and running.

Today, the remains of the running track at Olympia can still be seen. The shot put events at the 2004 Athens Olympics were held here.

TEST OF TIME

The marathon, a 26.2-mile (42.2 km) race, is based on an ancient Greek myth of a messenger who ran this distance to report the end of a war. However, it was not an event at the ancient Olympics. The marathon was invented in 1896 for the modern Olympic Games.

WOW!

The most extreme event at the ancient Olympics was pankration—a violent mixture of wrestling and boxing. There were almost no rules, but competitors couldn't bite each other or poke each other's eyes out!

This vase shows a pankration match. In pankration, competitors could kick, hit, and choke each other.

Gifts and glory

Athletes were motivated to take part in the Olympic Games to bring glory to their city-state. Although winners only received a laurel wreath at the Olympics, they returned home to fame and fortune. Their names were recorded and news of their victory, and that of their city-state, spread across the Greek world.

laurel leaves

29

GLOSSARY

acoustics How well sound can be heard in a place

Acropolis An ancient fortress in Athens

agora An official meeting place in ancient Greece

architecture The practice of designing and constructing buildings

astronomy The study of space, stars, and planets

cargo Goods carried by a ship or vehicle

chariot A horse-drawn vehicle used in ancient warfare and racing

city-state A city and the area around it that functions as an independent country

civilization The stage of a human society, such as its culture and way of life

colony An area controlled by another country

culture The beliefs and customs of a group of people

currency The system of money in a particular country

custom A habit or tradition

decomposed Decayed and gradually destroyed

democracy A system of government in which people vote and have a say in how things are run

dimensions The measurements of something, such as height or length

eclipse When a planet passes through the shadow of another planet

European Renaissance A time in Europe, roughly from the 1300s to the 1600s, marked by progress in the arts and sciences

exchange To trade one currency for another

fertile Soil that is able to produce healthy crops

formation A formal arrangement of troops

innovation The creation of a new product, idea, or method

legacy Something handed down from the past

logical Based on reasonable thought

monarchy Rule of a monarch

myth An invented story related to history

natural resources Materials or substances from nature that can be used to earn money

oligarchy Rule of a few rich or powerful people

optical illusion A misleading image that tricks the eye

Panathenaic Games An athletic competition held every four years in ancient Greece, from 566 B.C.E. to approximately 400 C.E.

papyrus A tall, reed-like plant used to make paper

patron A person who provides financial support to a person or organization

Persian Empire An empire in Western Asia that lasted from 550 B.C.E. to 330 B.C.E.

pharaoh A king or queen in ancient Egypt

philosophy The study of thought and knowledge

Phoenician A Mediterranean civilization, from 1500 B.C.E. to 300 B.C.E., that created a writing system widely used by other cultures

randomly Describes something chosen without planning

relation When two or more things are connected or working together

stereotypical An oversimplified idea about someone or something

symmetry When something is the same on both sides

tactical Planning and organizing soldiers in war

tiered Something that has several layers

Trojan War A mythical war fought between the ancient Greeks and the Trojans

truce An agreement to stop fighting for a time

TIMELINE

3000 to 1450 B.C.E.	The Minoan civilization develops on the island of Crete
1650 to 1100 B.C.E.	The Mycenaean civilization lives on mainland Greece
1100 to 800 B.C.E.	The Greek Dark Ages
800 to 508 B.C.E.	The Archaic period
776 B.C.E.	The first Olympic Games are held at Olympia
508 to 323 B.C.E.	The Classical period
508 B.C.E.	The first democracy is set up in Athens
431 to 404 B.C.E.	The Peloponnesian War takes place between Athens and Sparta
334 B.C.E.	Alexander the Great begins to conquer territories as part of his empire
323 B.C.E.	Alexander the Great dies
323 to 30 B.C.E.	The Hellenistic period

INDEX

LEARNING MORE

Websites

https://kids.nationalgeographic.com/explore/history/first-olympics/

www.historyforkids.net/ancient-greece.html

www.dkfindout.com/us/history/ancient-greece/

Books

Hudak, Heather C. *Forensic Investigations of the Ancient Greeks.* Crabtree Publishing, 2019.

Malam, John. *Ancient Greece Inside Out.* Crabtree Publishing, 2017.

Samuels, Charlie. *Ancient Greece.* Franklin Watts, 2015.